Twenty Love Poems

and a Song of Despair

Twenty Love Poems

and a Song of Despair

....

Pablo Neruda

Translation by W. S. Merwin
Foreword by Stephen Dobyns
Illustrations by Jan Thompson Dicks

CHRONICLE BOOKS
SAN FRANCISCO

Translated from the Spanish *Veinte poemas de amor y una canción desesperada.*
First published in Santiago de Chile, 1924. English language translation
copyright © 1969 by W.S. Merwin. Reprinted by arrangement with Viking
Penguin, a division of Penguin Books USA Inc.
Illustrations copyright © 1993 by Jan Thompson Dicks.
Compilation copyright © 1993 by Chronicle Books.

Illustrations: Jan Thompson Dicks
Book design: Gretchen Scoble
Cover design: Laura Lovett

Printed in Hong Kong.

Library of Congress Cataloging-in-Publication Data:

Neruda, Pablo, 1904–1973
[Veinte poemas de amor y una canción desesperada. English]
Twenty love poems and a song of despair / Pablo Neruda; translated by W.S.
Merwin; foreword by Stephen Dobyns; illustrations by Jan Thompson Dicks.
80 p.   133 x 184 cm.
ISBN 0-8118-0320-1
I. Merwin, W.S. (William Stanley), 1927–   II. Title.
PQ8097.N4V413   1993
861—dc20   92-45269
                                           CIP

Distributed in Canada by Raincoast Books
8680 Cambie Street, Vancouver, B.C. V6P 6M9

10 9 8 7

Chronicle Books
85 Second Street
San Francisco, CA 94105

Web Site: www.chronbooks.com

Contents

Stephen Dobyns

....

Veinte poemas de amor y una canción desesperada

A friend of mine, a Catalan poet, has told me that he once heard Pablo Neruda read his poetry in Venezuela in the 1960s to an audience of well over six hundred people. When Neruda finished, there were requests from the audience. The first was for Poem 20 from *Veinte poemas de amor y una canción desesperada*. The poem begins in W. S. Merwin's translation, "Tonight I can write the saddest lines" (*Puedo escribir los versos más tristes esta noche*). Neruda apologized. He had not brought that particular poem with him. "At which point," my friend said, "four hundred people stood up and recited the poem to him."

My wife, Isabel Bize, as a teenager in Santiago in the 1960s remembers how *Veinte poemas de amor* was devoured by all her friends, male and female. By then the book, first published in 1924, had sold two million copies. When a man gave flowers to a woman, he would often include several lines of one of the poems. And sometimes he would copy out a few lines to give instead of flowers. The slightly sentimental, slightly nostalgic tones of yearning and loss made the book required reading. It was discussed, wondered over, and dreamt with. Despite having been written in the twenties, it seemed of the moment, the language was the language being spoken right then within the city. Despite the aura of these being secret messages from the heart, a sort of hermetic longing, my wife and her friends felt no doubt about what the poems meant. They had no need for critics. The poems were being spoken directly to them.

Pablo Neruda was born Neftalí Ricardo Reyes Basoalto in Parral, a village about 200 miles south of Santiago, on July 12, 1904. His father worked for the railroad; his mother was a schoolteacher. A month after Neruda's birth his mother died of tuberculosis. In 1906 the family moved to Temuco, a small city another 200 miles south, and the father remarried. Neruda grew up in Temuco, a dusty frontier town in summer, a muddy one in winter when it would rain every day for three months. Despite his love for his stepmother and half-brothers and sisters, Neruda felt very different from them. He read voraciously, wrote poems and began translating Baudelaire at the age of twelve. His first poem appeared in a Santiago magazine when he was fourteen. Chile's other Nobel Prize-winning poet, Gabriela Mistral, happened to be principal of the girl's school in Temuco during this period. He would visit her (already he was president of the Temuco Literary Club) and she would lend him books, mostly Dostoyevski and Chekhov.

After graduation from high school in 1921, Neruda moved to Santiago and entered the Instituto Pedagógico in order to become a French teacher. By then he was widely published and had adopted the pseudonym Pablo Neruda (which he took from the Czech writer Jan Neruda), partly because he didn't want his poems to embarrass his family and perhaps influenced by Gabriela Mistral, who also wrote under a pseudonym (her name had been Lucila Godoy Alcayaga). Neruda strenuously lived the romantic life of a poet. He wore black and had a black cape. He wrote five poems a day. His friends were mostly bohemian artists, the shadier the better. He was passionate, he was energetic; he was seventeen.

In 1923 his first book, *Crepusculario,* was published by Claridad, the anarchist publication of the Chilean student federation. And he was already working on the poems in *Veinte poemas de amor.* For these poems he chose Chile's most successful publisher, Jorge Nascimento. But then came problems. Magazines rejected the new love poems and when Nascimento received the completed manuscript, he turned it down. The book was too raw, too sexual. Other publishers rejected the poems as well. Then an influential friend took the book back to Nascimento who reluctantly agreed to publish it. In 1924 *Veinte poemas de amor* came out in an edition of 500 to bad reviews and bad talk. So much so that Neruda felt obliged to publish an open letter in Santiago's *La Nación* (August 20, 1924) to defend himself:

> I undertook the greatest departure from myself: creation, wanting to illuminate words. Ten years of solitary labor, exactly half my life, have made diverse rhythms and contrary currents succeed one another in my expression. Grasping them, weaving them together, without ever finding the endurable element, because it does not exist, there you have my *Veinte poemas de amor y una canción desesperada.* Disperse as thought in its elusive variation, happy and sad, I have made these poems and I have suffered much in making them. [1]

Historically, the track record of literary critics is poor. Sainte-Beuve's condemnations of Baudelaire, Skabichevsky's condemnations of Chekhov, one wonders why critics are kept around. Despite the bad reviews, *Veinte poemas de amor* became immensely popular.

There followed the long life and great successes: four consular positions in the Far East; consular positions in Buenos Aires and Barcelona; Madrid during the Spanish Civil War and his conversion

8

to Communism; Neruda's return to Chile and his election as senator; his persecution by President González Videla; his flight from arrest and life underground as he finished his great *Canto General;* his return in 1952 and all the prizes and acclaim; his activities in Chilean politics culminating in his decision to run for president in the late 1960s as a Communist; his decision to step aside for his friend Salvador Allende; his ambassadorship to Paris under the Allende government; the Nobel Prize in 1971; his death in Santiago from cancer on September 23, 1973, in the midst of the bloody coup of General Augusto Pinochet, a coup bought and paid for by Henry Kissinger and the United States government.

During his long public life, Neruda was first of all a poet. His poems, too, were part of his public life, especially those he wrote after his conversion to Communism when he committed himself to clarity and to the constant articulation of the question: How does one live? One is struck by the changes from book to book, how Neruda took one style after another, yet always the books are rich in image and filled with exuberant energy. Near him when he wrote he kept three photographs: Whitman, Baudelaire, and Rimbaud. These poets were his teachers. Addressing members of PEN in New York City in April, 1972, Neruda said:

> Greatness has many faces, but I, a poet who writes in Spanish, learned more from Walt Whitman than from Cervantes. In Whitman's poetry, the ignorant are never humbled, and the human condition is never derided. [2]

The beginning of this journey is *Veinte poemas de amor.* In writing them, Neruda balanced a Symbolism partly influenced by the Nicaraguan poet Rubén Darío and an avant-garde poetry influenced by Apollinaire and the Chilean poet Vincente Huidobro. But Neruda had also been reading Rabindranath Tagore and admitted that his Poem XVI was a paraphrase of a Tagore poem. Some of the poems are formal compositions, some are in free verse. All are youthful, ardent, and breathless. *Veinte poemas de amor* was new. It belonged to the twentieth century and it belonged to South America. No European could have written it.

When he was fifty, Neruda told how the woman in *Veinte poemas de amor* was based on two women. And later still he named the country girl *Marisol* (sea and sun) and the city girl *Marisombra* (sea and shadow).

> *Marisol* is the idyll of the enchanted province, with immense evening stars and dark eyes like the wet sky of Temuco. She figures with her happiness and her lively legend, in nearly all the pages surrounded by the waters of the port and by the half moon over the mountains. *Marisombra* is the student of the capital. Gray cap, soft eyes, the constant scent of honeysuckle of our nomadic student love. The calm of passionate encounters in the hideaways of the city.[3]

Shortly after Neruda's death an edition of one hundred-and-eleven purloined love letters appeared in Madrid. Written between 1921 and 1931, they made it clear that Marisombra was Albertina Rosa Azócar Soto, a fellow student at El Instituto Pedagógico. The story goes that Neruda's one complaint about her was that she was always late. They would agree to meet on a street corner and for over an hour Neruda would hang about looking at his watch. Then, in 1927, when Neruda was on his way to Rangoon to serve as honorary consul, they decided to meet in Paris. Neruda kept the appointment. Thirty years later, he wrote about it in the poem "Forgotten in autumn" (*Olvido en otoño*), which begins

> It was half past seven
> in autumn
> and I was waiting
> for someone or other.
> Time, tired of being there with me,
> little by little left
> and left me alone.

He speaks of being humiliated by dogs, cats and policemen, of feeling more alone than ever in his life, until loneliness overwhelmed all other feelings and he could wait no longer.

> Later I fled from that
> insane corner,
> walking as quickly as possible,
> as if running away from the night,
> from a black and rolling boulder.
> What I am telling is nothing,
> but it happened to me once while
>   I was waiting
> for someone or other.[4]

Shortly after Neruda left, Albertina, the girl with the gray beret, arrived out of breath. Something important had come up and she had been delayed. But it was too late. Neruda was already on his way to Marseilles where he would catch the boat for Burma.

1. Quoted in *The Poetry of Pablo Neruda,* René de Costa, Harvard University Press, 1979, p. 21.
2. Pablo Neruda, *Passions and Impressions,* Farrar, Straus and Giroux, 1983, p. 377.
3. Quoted in de Costa, p. 26.
4. Pablo Neruda, *Extravagaria,* translated by Alastair Reid, Farrar, Straus and Giroux, 1974, pp. 126–129.

Twenty Love Poems

and a Song of Despair

B o d y   o f   a   W o m a n

Body of a woman, white hills, white thighs,

you look like a world, lying in surrender.

My rough peasant's body digs in you

and makes the son leap from the depth of the earth.

I was alone like a tunnel. The birds fled from me,

and night swamped me with its crushing invasion.

To survive myself I forged you like a weapon,

like an arrow in my bow, a stone in my sling.

But the hour of vengeance falls, and I love you.

Body of skin, of moss, of eager and firm milk.

Oh the goblets of the breast! Oh the eyes of absence!

Oh the roses of the pubis! Oh your voice, slow and sad!

Body of my woman, I will persist in your grace.

My thirst, my boundless desire, my shifting road!

Dark river-beds where the eternal thirst flows

and weariness follows, and the infinite ache.

☾

The Light Wraps You

The light wraps you in its mortal flame.

Abstracted pale mourner, standing that way

against the old propellers of the twilight

that revolves around you.

Speechless, my friend,

alone in the loneliness of this hour of the dead

and filled with the lives of fire,

pure heir of the ruined day.

A bough of fruit falls from the sun on your dark garment.

The great roots of night

grow suddenly from your soul,

and the things that hide in you come out again

so that a blue and pallid people,

your newly born, takes nourishment.

Oh magnificent and fecund and magnetic slave

of the circle that moves in turn through black and gold:

rise, lead and possess a creation

so rich in life that its flowers perish

and it is full of sadness.

☾

Ah   Vastness   of   Pines

Ah vastness of pines, murmur of waves breaking,

slow play of lights, solitary bell,

twilight falling in your eyes, toy doll,

earth-shell, in whom the earth sings!

In you the rivers sing and my soul flees in them

as you desire, and you send it where you will.

Aim my road on your bow of hope

and in a frenzy I will free my flock of arrows.

On all sides I see your waist of fog,

and your silence hunts down my afflicted hours;

my kisses anchor, and my moist desire nests

in you with your arms of transparent stone.

Ah your mysterious voice that love tolls and darkens

in the resonant and dying evening!

Thus in deep hours have I seen, over the fields,

the ears of wheat tolling in the mouth of the wind.

☾

IV

....

The Morning Is Full

The morning is full of storm

in the heart of summer.

The clouds travel like white handkerchiefs of goodbye,

the wind, travelling, waving them in its hands.

The numberless heart of the wind

beating above our loving silence.

Orchestral and divine, resounding among the trees

like a language full of wars and songs.

Wind that bears off the dead leaves with a quick raid

and deflects the pulsing arrows of the birds.

Wind that topples her in a wave without spray

and substance without weight, and leaning fires.

Her mass of kisses breaks and sinks,

assailed in the door of the summer's wind.

☾

V

So That You Will Hear Me

So that you will hear me

my words

sometimes grow thin

as the tracks of the gulls on the beaches.

Necklace, drunken bell

for your hands smooth as grapes.

And I watch my words from a long way off.

They are more yours than mine.

They climb on my old suffering like ivy.

It climbs the same way on damp walls.

You are to blame for this cruel sport.

They are fleeing from my dark lair.

You fill everything, you fill everything.

Before you they peopled the solitude that you occupy,

and they are more used to my sadness than you are.

Now I want them to say what I want to say to you

to make you hear as I want you to hear me.

The wind of anguish still hauls on them as usual.

Sometimes hurricanes of dreams still knock them over.

You listen to other voices in my painful voice.

Lament of old mouths, blood of old supplications.

Love me, companion. Don't forsake me. Follow me.

Follow me, companion, on this wave of anguish.

But my words become stained with your love.

You occupy everything, you occupy everything.

I am making them into an endless necklace

for your white hands, smooth as grapes.

☾

....

VI

I Remember You as You Were

I remember you as you were in the last autumn.

You were the grey beret and the still heart.

In your eyes the flames of the twilight fought on.

And the leaves fell in the water of your soul.

Clasping my arms like a climbing plant

the leaves garnered your voice, that was slow and at peace.

Bonfire of awe in which my thirst was burning.

Sweet blue hyacinth twisted over my soul.

I feel your eyes travelling, and the autumn is far off:

grey beret, voice of a bird, heart like a house

towards which my deep longings migrated

and my kisses fell, happy as embers.

Sky from a ship. Field from the hills:

Your memory is made of light, of smoke, of a still pond!

Beyond your eyes, farther on, the evenings were blazing.

Dry autumn leaves revolved in your soul.

☾

VII
....

Leaning into the Afternoons

Leaning into the afternoons I cast my sad nets

towards your oceanic eyes.

There in the highest blaze my solitude lengthens and flames,

its arms turning like a drowning man's.

I send out red signals across your absent eyes

that move like the sea near a lighthouse.

You keep only darkness, my distant female,

from your regard sometimes the coast of dread emerges.

Leaning into the afternoons I fling my sad nets

to that sea that beats on your marine eyes.

The birds of night peck at the first stars

that flash like my soul when I love you.

The night gallops on its shadowy mare

shedding blue tassels over the land.

☾

VIII

....

White Bee

White bee, you buzz in my soul, drunk with honey,

and your flight winds in slow spirals of smoke.

I am the one without hope, the word without echoes,

he who lost everything and he who had everything.

Last hawser, in you creaks my last longing.

In my barren land you are the final rose.

Ah you who are silent!

Let your deep eyes close. There the night flutters.

Ah your body, a frightened statue, naked.

You have deep eyes in which the night flails.

Cool arms of flowers and a lap of rose.

Your breasts seem like white snails.

A butterfly of shadow has come to sleep on your belly.

Ah you who are silent!

Here is the solitude from which you are absent.

It is raining. The sea wind is hunting stray gulls.

The water walks barefoot in the wet streets.

From that tree the leaves complain as though they were sick.

White bee, even when you are gone you buzz in my soul

You live again in time, slender and silent.

Ah you who are silent!

☾

IX

Drunk with Pines

Drunk with pines and long kisses,

like summer I steer the fast sail of the roses,

bent towards the death of the thin day,

stuck into my solid marine madness.

Pale and lashed to my ravenous water,

I cruise in the sour smell of the naked climate,

still dressed in grey and bitter sounds

and a sad crest of abandoned spray.

Hardened by passions, I go mounted on my one wave,

lunar, solar, burning and cold, all at once,

becalmed in the throat of the fortunate Isles

that are white and sweet as cool hips.

In the moist night my garment of kisses trembles

charged to insanity with electric currents,

heroically divided into dreams

and intoxicating roses practising on me.

Upstream, in the midst of the outer waves,

your parallel body yields to my arms

like a fish infinitely fastened to my soul,

quick and slow, in the energy under the sky.

☾

X
....

We Have Lost Even

We have lost even this twilight.

No one saw us this evening hand in hand

while the blue night dropped on the world.

I have seen from my window

the fiesta of sunset in the distant mountain tops.

Sometimes a piece of sun

burned like a coin between my hands.

I remembered you with my soul clenched

in that sadness of mine that you know.

Where were you then?

Who else was there?

Saying what?

Why will the whole of love come on me suddenly

when I am sad and feel you are far away?

The book fell that is always turned to at twilight

and my cape rolled like a hurt dog at my feet.

Always, always you recede through the evenings

towards where the twilight goes erasing statues.

☾

. . . .

XI

Almost   Out   of   the   Sky

Almost out of the sky, half of the moon

anchors between two mountains.

Turning, wandering night, the digger of eyes.

Let's see how many stars are smashed in the pool.

It makes a cross of mourning between my eyes, and runs away.

Forge of blue metals, nights of stilled combats,

my heart revolves like a crazy wheel.

Girl who have come from so far, been brought from so far,

sometimes your glance flashes out under the sky.

Rumbling, storm, cyclone of fury,

you cross above my heart without stopping.

Wind from the tombs carries off, wrecks, scatters your sleepy root.

The big trees on the other side of her, uprooted.

But you, cloudless girl, question of smoke, corn tassel.

You were what the wind was making with illuminated leaves.

Behind the nocturnal mountains, white lily of conflagration,

ah, I can say nothing! You were made of everything.

Longing that sliced my breast into pieces,

it is time to take another road, on which she does not smile.

Storm that buried the bells, muddy swirl of torments,

why touch her now, why make her sad.

Oh to follow the road that leads away from everything,

without anguish, death, winter waiting along it

with their eyes open through the dew.

☾

XII

Your Breast Is Enough

Your breast is enough for my heart,

and my wings for your freedom.

What was sleeping above your soul will rise

out of my mouth to heaven.

In you is the illusion of each day.

You arrive like the dew to the cupped flowers.

You undermine the horizon with your absence.

Eternally in flight like the wave.

I have said that you sang in the wind

like the pines and like the masts.

Like them you are tall and taciturn,

and you are sad, all at once, like a voyage.

You gather things to you like an old road.

You are peopled with echoes and nostalgic voices.

I awoke and at times birds fled and migrated

that had been sleeping in your soul.

☾

XIII

....

I Have Gone Marking

I have gone marking the atlas of your body

with crosses of fire.

My mouth went across: a spider, trying to hide.

In you, behind you, timid, driven by thirst.

Stories to tell you on the shore of evening,

sad and gentle doll, so that you should not be sad.

A swan, a tree, something far away and happy.

The season of grapes, the ripe and fruitful season.

I who lived in a harbour from which I loved you.

The solitude crossed with dream and with silence.

Penned up between the sea and sadness.

Soundless, delirious, between two motionless gondoliers.

Between the lips and the voice something goes dying.

Something with the wings of a bird, something of anguish and oblivion.

The way nets cannot hold water

My toy doll, only a few drops are left trembling.

Even so, something sings in these fugitive words.

Something sings, something climbs to my ravenous mouth.

Oh to be able to celebrate you with all the words of joy.

Sing, burn, flee, like a belfry at the hands of a madman.

My sad tenderness, what comes over you all at once?

When I have reached the most awesome and the coldest summit

my heart closes like a nocturnal flower.

☾

XIV
....

Every Day You Play

Every day you play with the light of the universe.

Subtle visitor, you arrive in the flower and the water.

You are more than this white head that I hold tightly

as a cluster of fruit, every day, between my hands.

You are like nobody since I love you.

Let me spread you out among yellow garlands.

Who writes your name in letters of smoke among the stars of the south?

Oh let me remember you as you were before you existed.

Suddenly the wind howls and bangs at my shut window.

The sky is a net crammed with shadowy fish.

Here all the winds let go sooner or later, all of them.

The rain takes off her clothes.

The birds go by, fleeing.

The wind. The wind.

I can contend only against the power of men.

The storm whirls dark leaves

and turns loose all the boats that were moored last night to the sky.

You are here. Oh, you do not run away.

You will answer me to the last cry.

Cling to me as though you were frightened.

Even so, at one time a strange shadow ran through your eyes.

Now, now too, little one, you bring me honeysuckle,

and even your breasts smell of it.

While the sad wind goes slaughtering butterflies

I love you, and my happiness bites the plum of your mouth.

How you must have suffered getting accustomed to me,

my savage, solitary soul, my name that sends them all running.

So many times we have seen the morning star burn, kissing our eyes,

and over our heads the grey light unwinds in turning fans.

My words rained over you, stroking you.

A long time I have loved the sunned mother-of-pearl of your body.

I go so far as to think that you own the universe.

I will bring you happy flowers from the mountains, bluebells,

dark hazels, and rustic baskets of kisses.

I want

to do with you what spring does with the cherry trees.

☾

XV

I Like for You to Be Still

I like for you to be still: it is as though you were absent,

and you hear me from far away and my voice does not touch you.

It seems as though your eyes had flown away

and it seems that a kiss had sealed your mouth.

As all things are filled with my soul

you emerge from the things, filled with my soul.

You are like my soul, a butterfly of dream,

and you are like the word Melancholy.

I like for you to be still, and you seem far away.

It sounds as though you were lamenting, a butterfly cooing like a dove.

And you hear me from far away, and my voice does not reach you:

Let me come to be still in your silence.

And let me talk to you with your silence

that is bright as a lamp, simple as a ring.

You are like the night, with its stillness and constellations.

Your silence is that of a star, as remote and candid.

I like for you to be still: it is as though you were absent,

distant and full of sorrow as though you had died.

One word then, one smile, is enough.

And I am happy, happy that it's not true.

☽

XVI

....

In My Sky at Twilight

This poem is a paraphrase of the 30th poem in Rabindranath Tagore's The Gardener.

In my sky at twilight you are like a cloud

and your form and colour are the way I love them.

You are mine, mine, woman with sweet lips

and in your life my infinite dreams live.

The lamp of my soul dyes your feet,

My sour wine is sweeter on your lips,

oh reaper of my evening song,

how solitary dreams believe you to be mine!

You are mine, mine, I go shouting it to the afternoon's

wind, and the wind hauls on my widowed voice.

Huntress of the depths of my eyes, your plunder

stills your nocturnal regard as though it were water.

You are taken in the net of my music, my love,

and my nets of music are wide as the sky.

My soul is born on the shore of your eyes of mourning.

In your eyes of mourning the land of dreams begins.

☾

XVII

Thinking, Tangling Shadows

Thinking, tangling shadows in the deep solitude.

You are far away too, oh farther than anyone.

Thinking, freeing birds, dissolving images,

burying lamps.

Belfry of fogs, how far away, up there!

Stifling laments, milling shadowy hopes,

taciturn miller,

night falls on you face downward, far from the city.

Your presence is foreign, as strange to me as a thing.

I think, I explore great tracts of my life before you.

My life before anyone, my harsh life.

The shout facing the sea, among the rocks,

running free, mad, in the sea-spray.

The sad rage, the shout, the solitude of the sea.

Headlong, violent, stretched towards the sky.

You, woman, what were you there, what ray, what vane

of that immense fan? You were as far as you are now.

Fire in the forest! Burn in blue crosses.

Burn, burn, flame up, sparkle in trees of light.

It collapses, crackling. Fire. Fire.

And my soul dances, seared with curls of fire.

Who calls? What silence peopled with echoes?

Hour of nostalgia, hour of happiness, hour of solitude,

hour that is mine from among them all!

Hunting horn through which the wind passes singing.

Such a passion of weeping tied to my body.

Shaking of all the roots,

attack of all the waves!

My soul wandered, happy, sad, unending.

Thinking, burying lamps in the deep solitude.

Who are you, who are you?

☾

....

XVIII

Here I Love You

Here I love you.

In the dark pines the wind disentangles itself.

The moon glows like phosphorus on the vagrant waters.

Days, all one kind, go chasing each other.

The snow unfurls in dancing figures.

A silver gull slips down from the west.

Sometimes a sail. High, high stars.

Oh the black cross of a ship.

Alone.

Sometimes I get up early and even my soul is wet.

Far away the sea sounds and resounds.

This is a port.

Here I love you.

Here I love you and the horizon hides you in vain.

I love you still among these cold things.

Sometimes my kisses go on those heavy vessels

that cross the sea towards no arrival.

I see myself forgotten like those old anchors.

The piers sadden when the afternoon moors there.

My life grows tired, hungry to no purpose.

I love what I do not have. You are so far.

My loathing wrestles with the slow twilights.

But night comes and starts to sing to me.

The moon turns its clockwork dream.

The biggest stars look at me with your eyes.

And as I love you, the pines in the wind

want to sing your name with their leaves of wire.

XIX

....

Girl Lithe and Tawny

Girl lithe and tawny, the sun that forms

the fruits, that plumps the grains, that curls seaweeds

filled your body with joy, and your luminous eyes

and your mouth that has the smile of the water.

A black yearning sun is braided into the strands

of your black mane, when you stretch your arms.

You play with the sun as with a little brook

and it leaves two dark pools in your eyes.

Girl lithe and tawny, nothing draws me towards you.

Everything bears me farther away, as though you were noon.

You are the frenzied youth of the bee,

the drunkenness of the wave, the power of the wheat-ear.

My sombre heart searches for you, nevertheless,

and I love your joyful body, your slender and flowing voice.

Dark butterfly, sweet and definitive

like the wheat-field and the sun, the poppy and the water.

☾

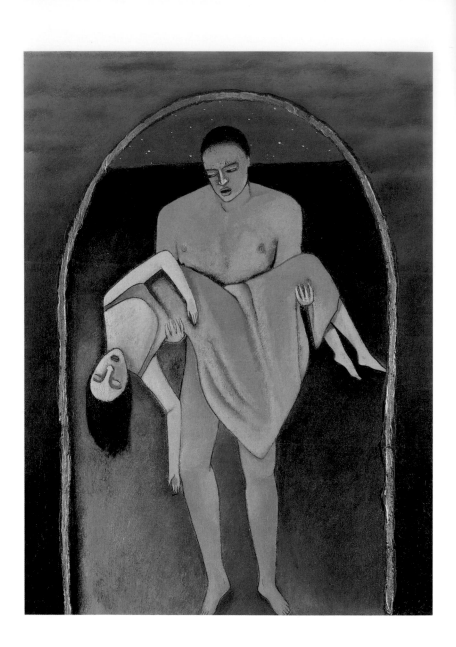

XX

....

Tonight I Can Write

Tonight I can write the saddest lines.

Write, for example, 'The night is starry

and the stars are blue and shiver in the distance.'

The night wind revolves in the sky and sings.

Tonight I can write the saddest lines.

I loved her, and sometimes she loved me too.

Through nights like this one I held her in my arms.

I kissed her again and again under the endless sky.

She loved me, sometimes I loved her too.

How could one not have loved her great still eyes.

Tonight I can write the saddest lines.

To think that I do not have her. To feel that I have lost her.

To hear the immense night, still more immense without her.

And the verse falls to the soul like dew to the pasture.

What does it matter that my love could not keep her.

The night is starry and she is not with me.

This is all. In the distance someone is singing. In the distance.

My soul is not satisfied that it has lost her.

My sight tries to find her as though to bring her closer.

My heart looks for her, and she is not with me.

The same night whitening the same trees.

We, of that time, are no longer the same.

I no longer love her, that's certain, but how I loved her.

My voice tried to find the wind to touch her hearing.

Another's. She will be another's. As she was before my kisses.

Her voice, her bright body. Her infinite eyes.

I no longer love her, that's certain, but maybe I love her.

Love is so short, forgetting is so long.

Because through nights like this one I held her in my arms

my soul is not satisfied that it has lost her.

Though this be the last pain that she makes me suffer

and these the last verses that I write for her.

The Song of Despair

The memory of you emerges from the night around me.

The river mingles its stubborn lament with the sea.

Deserted like the wharves at dawn.

It is the hour of departure, oh deserted one!

Cold flower heads are raining over my heart.

Oh pit of debris, fierce cave of the shipwrecked.

In you the wars and the flights accumulated.

From you the wings of the song birds rose.

You swallowed everything, like distance.

Like the sea, like time. In you everything sank!

It was the happy hour of assault and the kiss.

The hour of the spell that blazed like a lighthouse.

Pilot's dread, fury of a blind diver,

turbulent drunkenness of love, in you everything sank!

In the childhood of mist my soul, winged and wounded.

Lost discoverer, in you everything sank!

You girdled sorrow, you clung to desire,

sadness stunned you, in you everything sank!

I made the wall of shadow draw back,

beyond desire and act, I walked on.

Oh flesh, my own flesh, woman whom I loved and lost,

I summon you in the moist hour, I raise my song to you.

Like a jar you housed the infinite tenderness,

and the infinite oblivion shattered you like a jar.

There was the black solitude of the islands,

and there, woman of love, your arms took me in.

There were thirst and hunger, and you were the fruit.

There were grief and the ruins, and you were the miracle.

Ah woman, I do not know how you could contain me

in the earth of your soul, in the cross of your arms!

How terrible and brief was my desire of you!

How difficult and drunken, how tensed and avid.

Cemetery of kisses, there is still fire in your tombs,

still the fruited boughs burn, pecked at by birds.

Oh the bitten mouth, oh the kissed limbs,

oh the hungering teeth, oh the entwined bodies.

Oh the mad coupling of hope and force

in which we merged and despaired.

And the tenderness, light as water and as flour.

And the word scarcely begun on the lips.

This was my destiny and in it was the voyage of my longing,

and in it my longing fell, in you everything sank!

Oh pit of debris, everything fell into you,

what sorrow did you not express, in what sorrow are you not drowned!

From billow to billow you still called and sang.

Standing like a sailor in the prow of a vessel.

You still flowered in songs, you still broke in currents.

Oh pit of debris, open and bitter well.

Pale blind diver, luckless slinger,

lost discoverer, in you everything sank!

It is the hour of departure, the hard cold hour

which the night fastens to all the timetables.

The rustling belt of the sea girdles the shore.

Cold stars heave up, black birds migrate.

Deserted like the wharves at dawn.

Only the tremulous shadow twists in my hands.

Oh farther than everything. Oh farther than everything.

It is the hour of departure. Oh abandoned one.

☾